Coloring Book

ANIMALS
of
South America

Mark Shawe

Book Series: Animal Planet

In this Coloring Book you will find:

- 20 original realistic full-page images of wild animals of South America on single-sided sheets to prevent bleed-through
- 60 interesting unusual facts about the animals

Grab you favorite tool: pencils, crayons, markers or paints, and start coloring!

ISBN: 9781079222920

WORLD MAP

Howler monkey

These primates get their name from their unique, and quite loud, vocalizations. In fact, you can even hear this species howl from up to 3 miles away (almost 5,5 km). If you've ever watched these creatures climbing through the trees, you might have gotten a little confused trying to keep track of what's a hand and what's a tail. This is because these monkeys have prehensile tails, which means they can move their tails to grab the branches around them. These monkeys do not make good pets. In fact, no monkey species makes a good pet. These creatures have complex social and mental stimulation needs, and strict dietary restrictions.

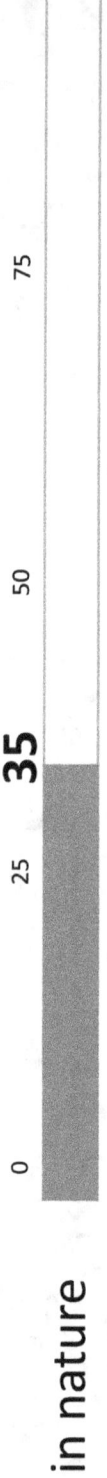

life expectancy in nature

weigh up to   6 kg (13 lb)

0   25   **35**   50   75   100

Puma

Puma is the largest of the small cat species. Pumas have a strong built, with large paws and sharp claws. Their hind legs are larger and more muscular than their front legs, which gives them great jumping power. One of the reasons as to why this beautiful feline is not classified as one of the world's 'big' cats is that pumas are not able to roar.

life expectancy in nature

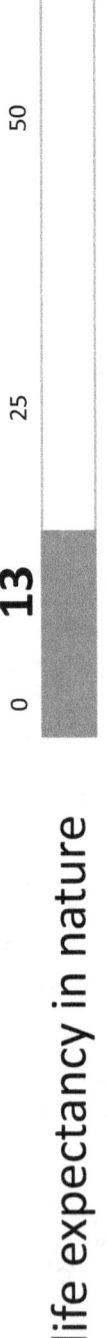

| 0 | **13** | 25 | 50 | 75 | 100 |

weigh up to   80 kg (176 lb)

Otter

Otters are adorable creatures that live both on land and in the water. They enjoy the freshwater but they are also known to live in the saltwater of the oceans as well. Otters like to throw and bounce things, wrestle, twirl, and chase their tail. They also play tag and chase each other, both in the water and on the ground. Beaver habitat is a great place to find otters, because the otters benefit from the dams and dens beavers build. Otters are a popular animal in Japanese folklore where they are called "kawauso". In these tales the smart kawauso often fool humans, like a fox.

life expectancy in nature

16

| 0 | 25 | 50 | 75 | 100 |

weigh up to   10 kg (22 lb)

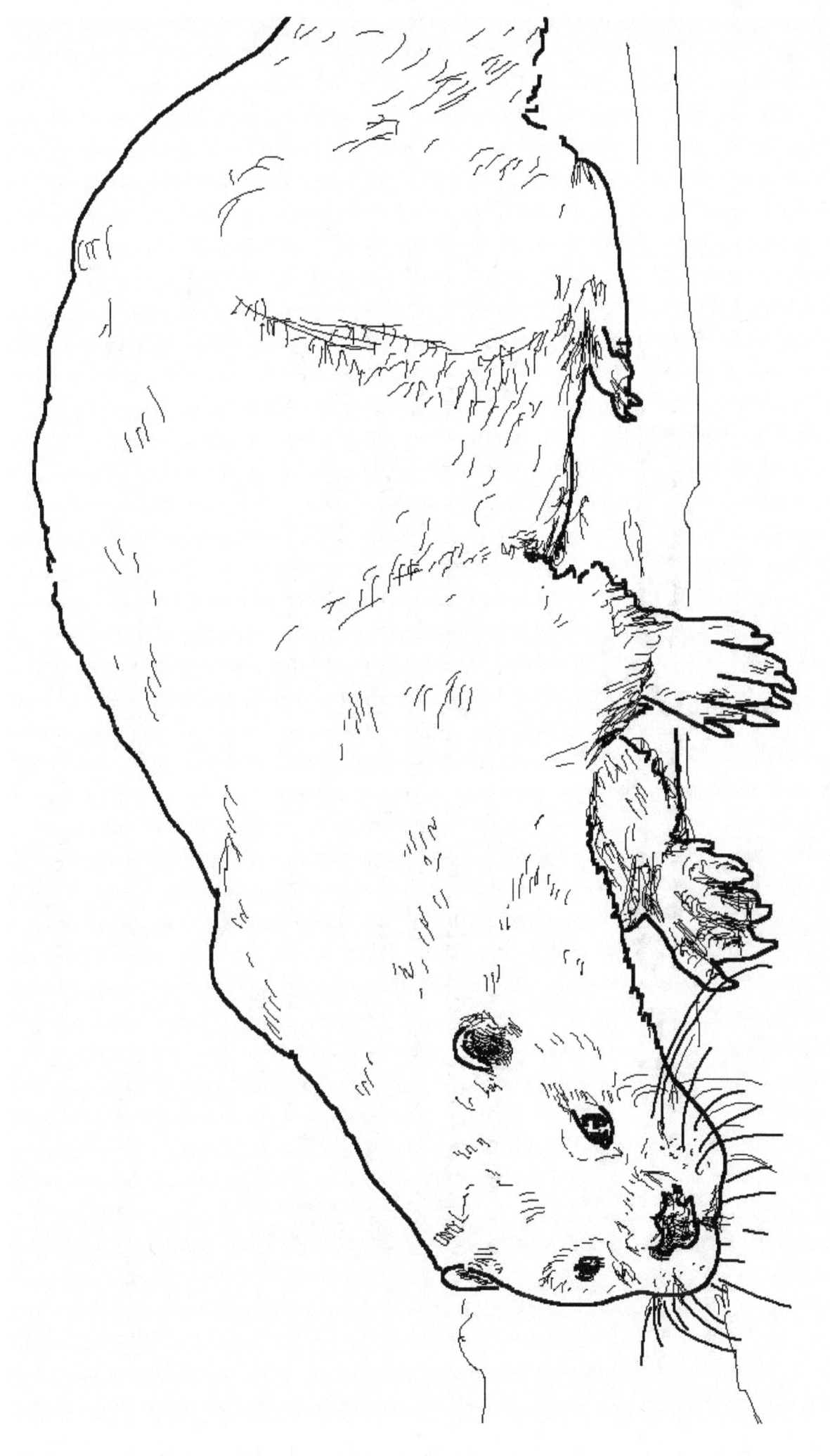

Galapagos tortoise

Unlike any other animal, Galapagos tortoise can survive up to one year without food and water. When the first Spanish sailors arrived to the island, they saw a large number of tortoises. Since tortoise is called "Galapago" in Spanish, the whole island is named Galapagos Island. Galapagos tortoises are cold-blooded animals (they don't have stable body temperature), because of that, Galapagos tortoises enjoy basking in the sun.

life expectancy in nature

0   50   100   **150**   200

weigh up to   300 kg (660 lb)

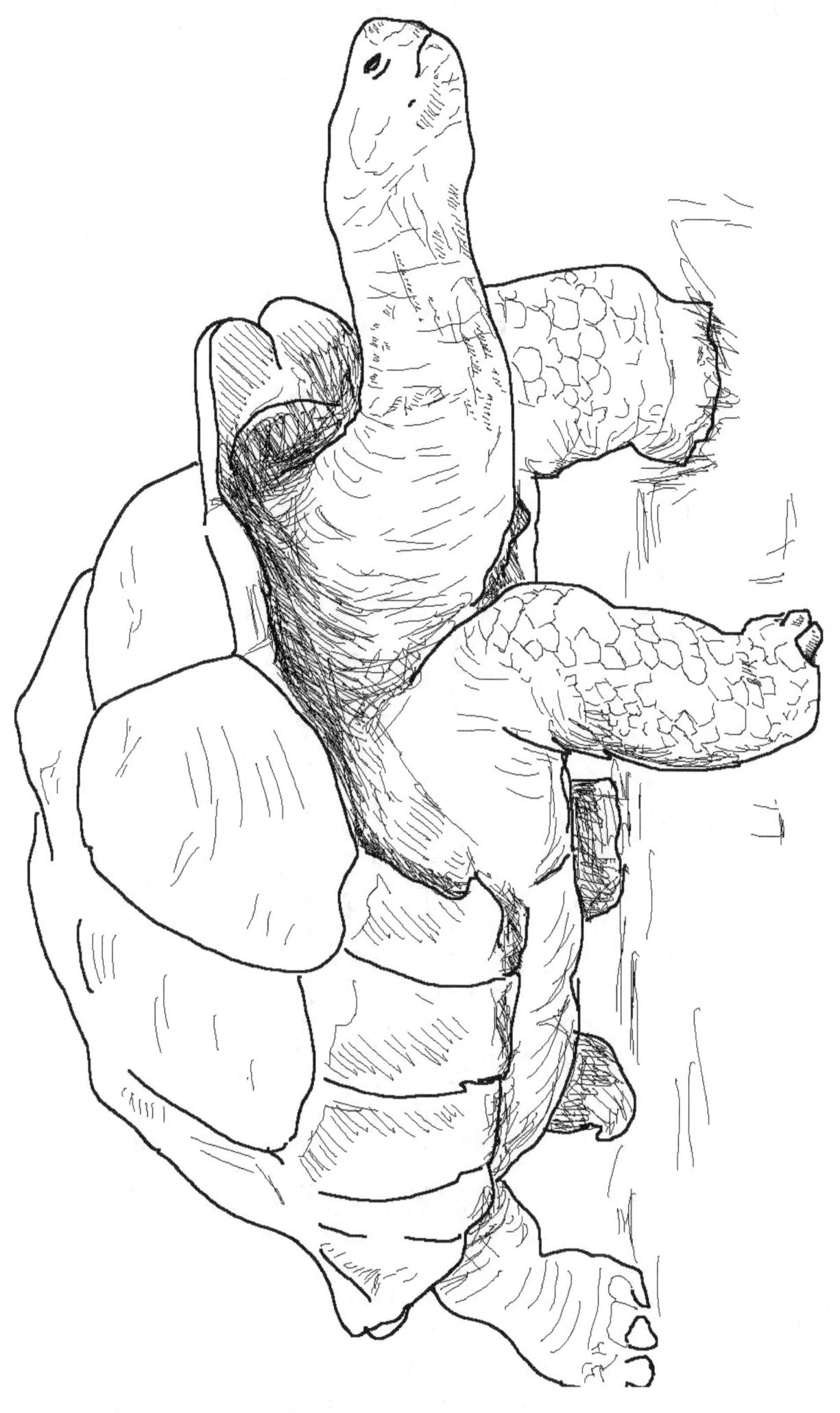

Alpaca

Alpacas communicate through body language. The most common is spitting when they are in distress, fearful, or mean to show dominance. Alpaca fiber is used for making knitted and woven items, same as the sheep's wool. The fiber comes in more than 52 natural colors. During the period of Incan civilization, the wearing of robes made of alpaca was reserved for the nobility and royalty.

life expectancy in nature

20

| 0 | 25 | 50 | 75 | 100 |

weigh up to   80 kg (176 lb)

Piranha

A piranha is a ferocious freshwater fish. The word piranha literally translates as "tooth fish" in the indigenous Brazilian language of Tupi. They need warm water to survive and don't eat when the water temperature is less than 12°C (54°F) degrees Fahrenheit. The total number of piranha species is unknown, and new species continue to be described. Various stories exist about piranhas, such as how they can dilacerate a human body or cattle in seconds. These usually refer to the red-bellied piranha.

life expectancy in nature

0	**10**	25	50	75	100

weigh up to   1 kg (2 lb)

Rhea

Rheas are tall, flightless birds. These birds are capable of reaching speeds up to 37 mph. While this isn't that impressive when you compare them to a cheetah (70 mph), or a pronghorn (55 mph), it still dwarfs a human's top speed! However, these birds aren't just sprinting around all the time. They prefer a leisurely cruise while searching for food. They are primarily herbivorous. Researchers have seen rheas eat snakes, small birds, fish, and other small creatures. Some people keep them on farms.

life expectancy in nature

10

0   25   50   75   100

weigh up to   150 kg (330 lb)

Anteater

Anteaters vary in size according to their species. The giant anteater is up to 2.1 meters (7 feet) long including the tail. All anteaters have protruding snouts equipped with a thin tongue that can be extended to a length greater than the length of the head. The anteater's tongue is covered with thousands of tiny hooks which are used to hold the insects together with large amounts of saliva. But it has to eat quickly, flicking its tongue up to 160 times per minute - ants fight back with painful stings, so an anteater may spend only a minute feasting on each mound.

life expectancy in nature

0   **15**   25   50   75   100

weigh up to   5 kg (11 lb)

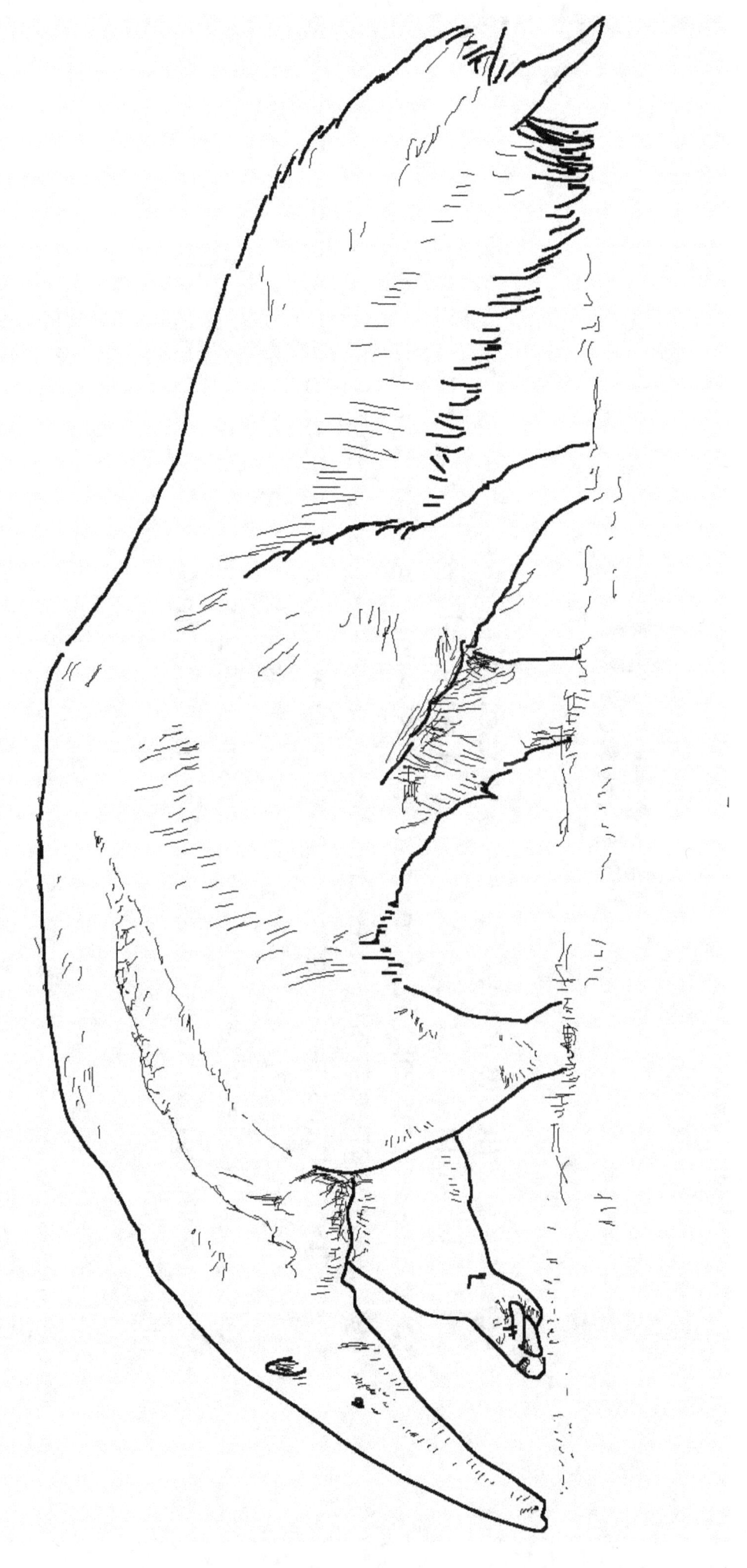

Agouti

Agoutis are equipped with sharp incisors that are able to crack the shell of Brazilian nut. Special layer of enamel provides extra strength that is required for breaking the hard shells. Brazilian nuts are one of agouti's favorite treats. Besides them, agouti eats fallen fruit, succulent plants and crabs. Agouti can recognize the sound when fruit is falling to the ground. Agouti sometimes acts like a gardener of forests. It stores the nuts and seeds in the ground to feast on later. Whenever agouti forgets about them, nuts and seeds grow into new plant.

life expectancy in nature

weigh up to   4 kg (9 lb)

Tapir

Although pig-like in appearance, their closest existing relatives are the horses and rhinoceroses. The tapir's nose and upper lip combine into a flexible snout like an elephant's trunk. They use it to grab leaves from the nearby branches, pick up the fruit from the ground or to find aquatic plant on the bottom of the water. When frightened, tapirs can take to the water and breathe with their snout poked above the surface like a snorkel.

life expectancy in nature

0   25 **30**   50   75   100

weigh up to   270 kg (595 lb)

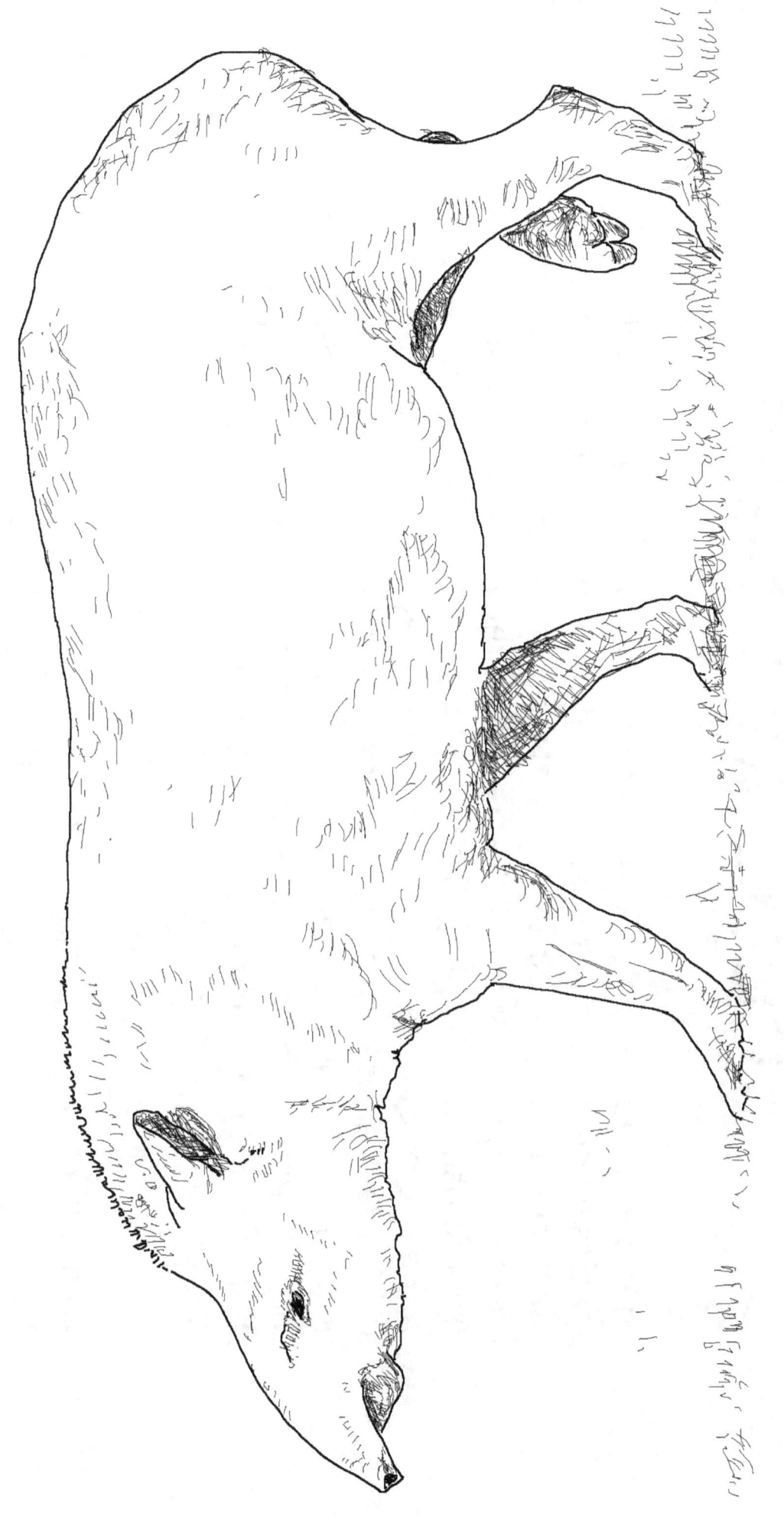

Spectacled bear

The spectacled bear, also known as the Andean bear is the only bear species living in South America. One of the more unique features of spectacled bears is their use of platforms or "nests" which the bears create in the understory of the trees that they browse in for fruit. They are also used for sleeping. The spectacled bear plays an important role in the ecology of the rain forest because they eat so much fruit. The seeds they eat are excreted in their droppings as the bears move around, spreading the seeds over long distances for the production of the next generation of fruit trees throughout the forest. Because of their tropical native climate, spectacled bears don't sleep in winter and are active year-round.

life expectancy in nature

weigh up to   155 kg (340 lb)

0   25   **25**   50   75   100

The maned wolf

The maned wolf is the largest canid of South America. It is neither a wolf, like its name, nor a fox, like its appearance. The maned wolf is not closely related to any other living canid. It is the tallest of the wild canids; its long legs are likely an adaptation to the tall grasslands of its native habitat. They are threatened by habitat loss and being run over by cars.

life expectancy in nature

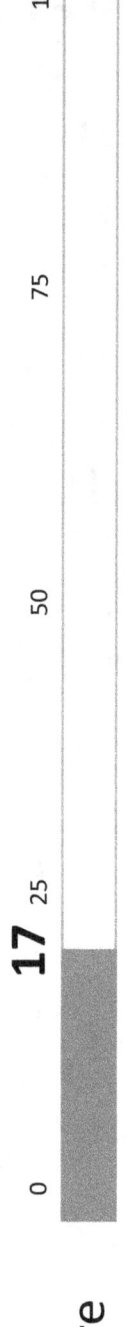

17

0   25   50   75   100

weigh up to   25 kg (55 lb)

Guanaco

Guanacos are the mostly widely distributed of the four species of lamoids and they occupy the most diverse range of habitats. Domesticated guanakos are called llamas. There are no llamas in the wild. Guanacos are not picky in food, they can survive on harsh brush and grasses in the wild. Its blood can carry more oxygen than other mammals, which helps the guanaco live well at altitudes of up to 4,000 meters (13,120 feet). They are also excellent swimmers.

life expectancy in nature

18

| 0 | 25 | 50 | 75 | 100 |

weigh up to   140 kg (305 lb)

Andean condor

Its habitat is mainly composed of open grasslands and alpine areas up to 5,000 meters (16,000 feet) in elevation. It prefers areas with wide open spaces which help in their detection of food. The Andean condor is one of the world's longest-living birds, with a lifespan of around 50 years in the wild. Andean condors are vultures. Like all vultures, they are carrion feeders, not predators. The Andean condor is a national symbol of Argentina, Bolivia, Chile, Colombia, Ecuador, Peru and Venezuelan Andes states. It has also appeared on the coins and banknotes of Colombia and Chile. The condor is featured in several coats of arms of Andean countries as a symbol of the Andes Mountains.

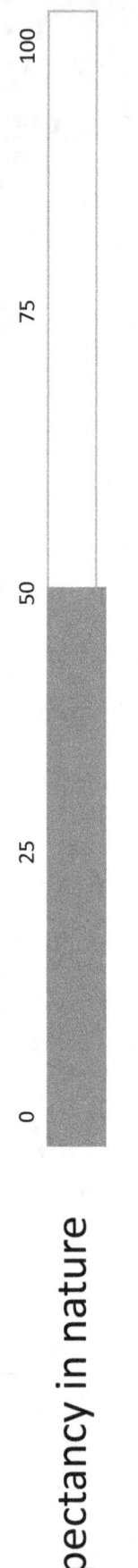

50

life expectancy in nature

weigh up to   15 kg (33 lb)

Hercules beetle

Some reports have indicated the Hercules beetle can carry up to 850 times its body mass. Hercules beetles are found only in Central and South America, but they are bred and kept as pets in many countries around the world. When males fight with each other to gain mating rights with females, they use their pincers to pick up their opponents and smash them to the ground. Rearing Hercules beetles can be very challenging, but can be done with specialist knowledge. They can be housed in a standard aquarium.

life expectancy in nature

2

0   25   50   75   100

weigh up to   0.1 kg (0.22 lb)

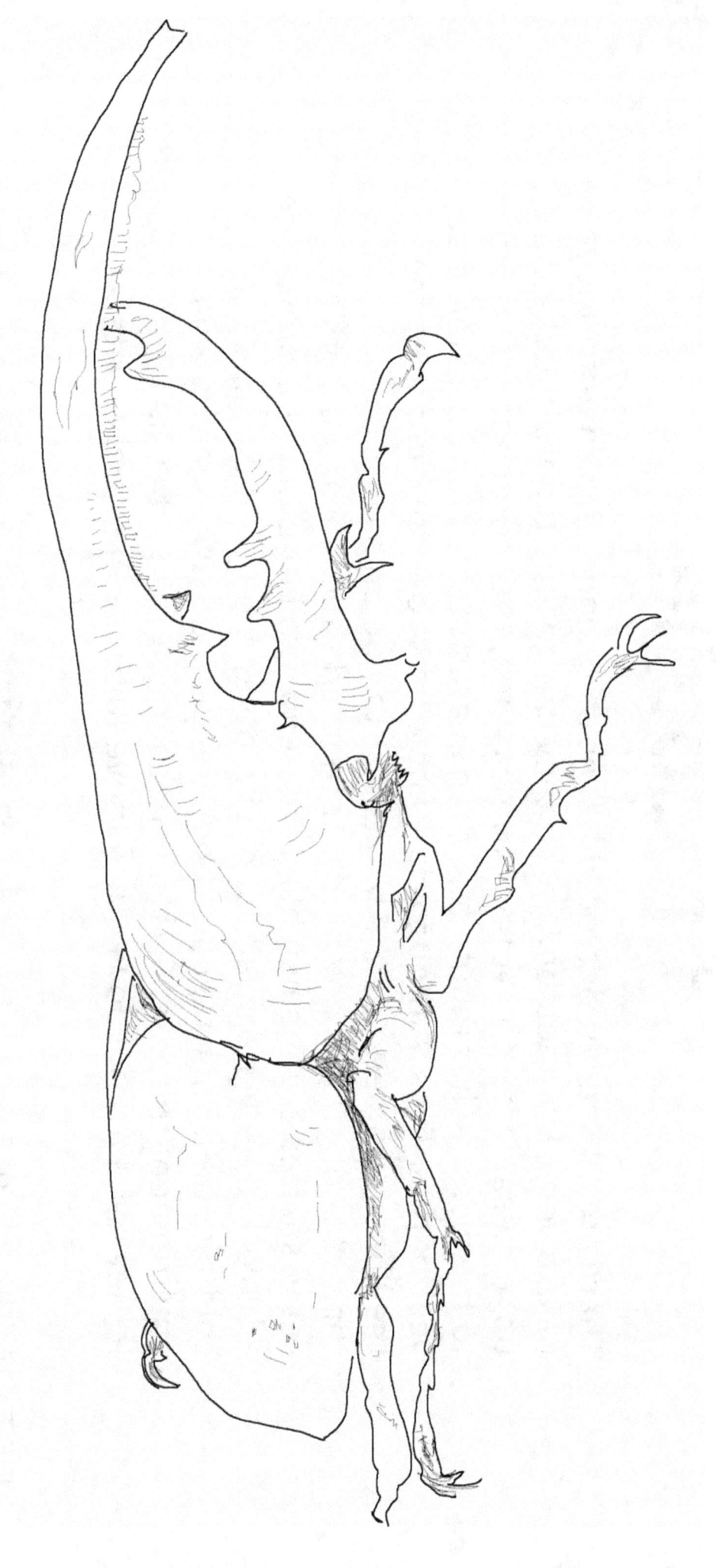

Crocodile

There are 14 species of crocodiles. As cold-blooded predators, they have a very slow metabolism, so they can go long time without food – up to a year. After the young have hatched, the mother carries them to the water in her mouth and then guards them for most of the first year of their lives. Although they know how to swim from the time they hatch, sometimes the babies get to ride on mom's back, too. She threatens or attacks any predator that lurks too close; mothers of some species call the hatchlings to swim into her mouth for protection – looks like they are swallowed! Like other reptiles, crocodiles are cold-blooded. They regulate body temperature by changing what environment they are in. If they need to warm up, they lie in the sun. If they need to cool down, they move to shade or into the water.

life expectancy in nature

80

weigh up to   100 kg (220 lb)

Black racer

Southern black racers are not venomous. Instead of using venom, these snakes prefer to crush their prey into the ground and swallow it whole. As they are very active in the daytime and less afraid of humans than most snakes, it is fairly common to see these snakes in suburban yards. .

life expectancy in nature

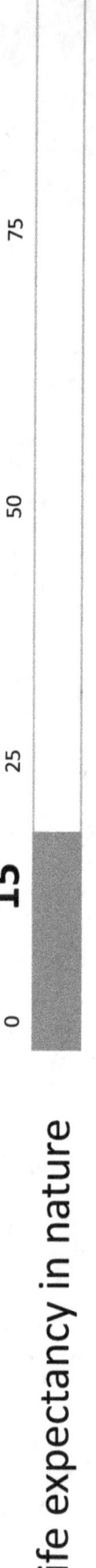

0   15   25   50   75   100

weigh up to   1.5 kg (3.3 lb)

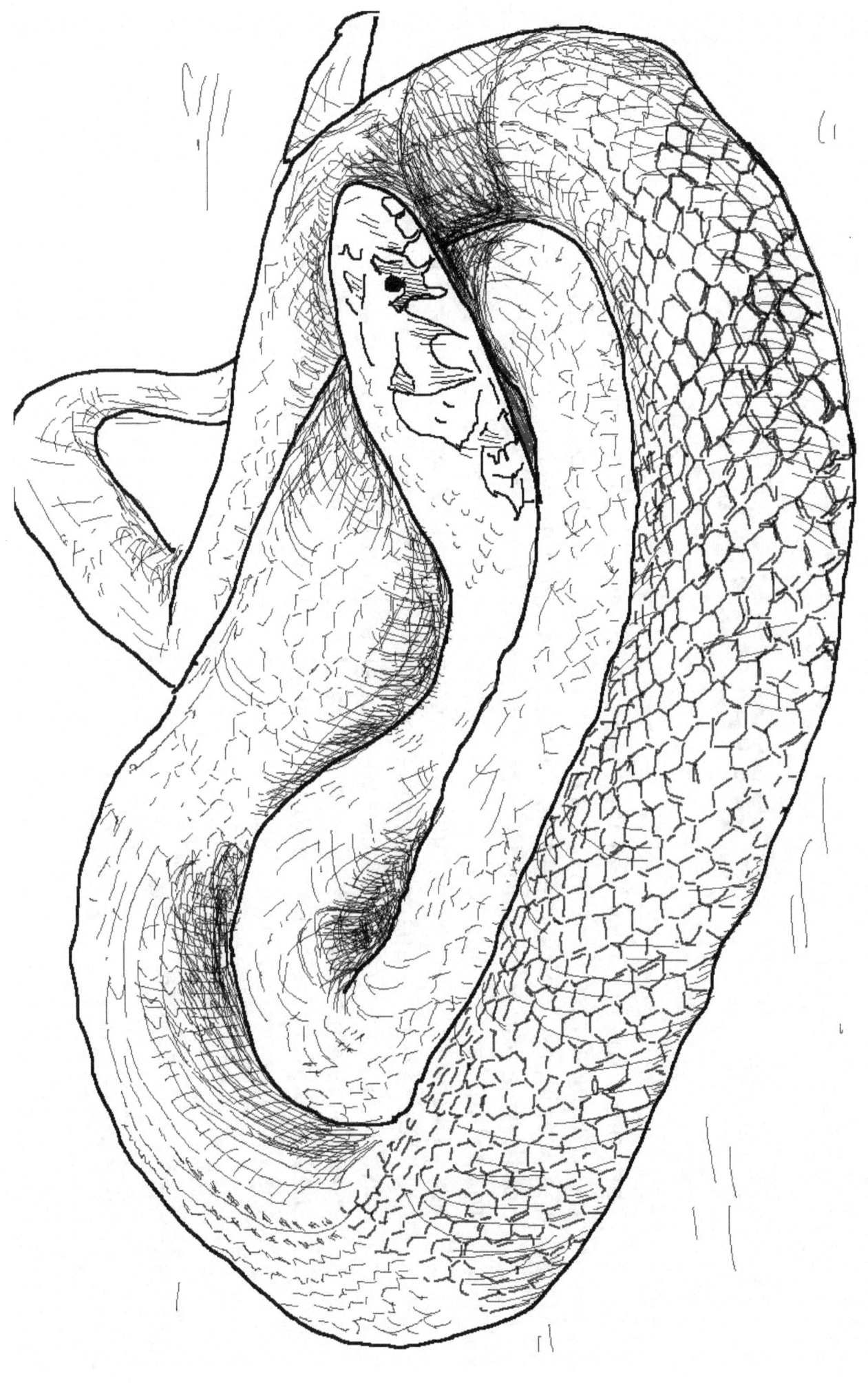

Cane toad

They are also known as "marine toads," and "giant neotropical" toads. If you are craving a late-night snack, a cane toad is a poor choice. Unfortunately, many animals don't realize this. Outside of their natural range in Central and South America, cane toads have few predators. This is because of their deadly toxin, bufotenin. Cane toads hunt by tracking movement. Actually, if it is small enough to fit in its mouth, and it moves, the cane toad will eat it. People introduced cane toads to a number of different locations before realizing their mistake. These invasive species were originally intended to eat other pests. However, even though they were successful at reducing pest populations, they caused native fauna to suffer. Nowadays scientists are working to combat the invasive populations.

life expectancy in nature

6

0   25   50   75   100

weigh up to   2 kg (4,5 lb)

Anaconda

Although the name 'anaconda' applies to all four species of anacondas, it is often used in reference to only the green anaconda which is the largest snake in the world by weight, and the second longest. In all species females are larger than males. An anaconda kills its prey by coiling its muscular body around the creature and squeezing until the animal can no longer breathe. Jaws attached by stretchy ligaments allow them to swallow their prey whole, no matter the size. The interesting fact is that anacondas produce eggs but incubate them internally, females typically have around 30 babies. Newborn anacondas are smaller versions of the adults and instinctively know how to survive on their own without any help from their mother.

life expectancy in nature

| 0 | 25 | **55** | 50 | 75 | 100 |

weigh up to   100 kg (220 lb)

Ocelot

The ocelot also known as the dwarf leopard, is a wild cat. Ocelots live primarily in the rain forests of South America. Like all small cats, ocelots have very good vision and hearing. Their eyes have a special layer that collects light. When they're ready to eat, the wild cats don't chew their food—instead they use their teeth to tear meat into pieces and then swallow it whole. At one point, more than 200,000 ocelots per year were killed for their coats. Today, with laws prohibiting hunting for the fur trade, there are no ocelot coats for sale, and the "pet" ocelot is history.

14

0	25	50	75	100

life expectancy in nature

weigh up to   16 kg (35 lb)

Dear Reader!

Thank you for choosing my book! Hope you enjoyed it!

If you really liked it, please, **leave a short review on Amazon!**
Use ISBN # 9781079222920 to find this book

Check out my website http://21centurywritersclub.com/ for more
books by me and my fellow writers!

See ya,
Mark

SEARCH MORE COLORING BOOKS

Book Series: Animal Planet

Animals of Europe

ISBN # 9781079222258

Animals of North America

ISBN # 9781079225525

Animals of Africa

ISBN # 9781079227536

Animals of Asia

ISBN # 9781079224740

Animals of Antarctica

ISBN # 9781079225969

Animals of Australia

ISBN # 9781079226393

SPECIAL EDITION

COLORING BOOK:
ANIMALS OF THE WORLD

140 original realistic full-page images of wild animals of the World on single-sided sheets to prevent bleed-through

420 interesting unusual facts about the animals

COLORING BOOK
ANIMALS OF THE WORLD
140 drawings

Mark Shawe

140 realistic pictures + 420 unique facts about animals

BEST SELLER · BEST SELLER · No.1 · BEST SELLER

ISBN # 9781079226799

Book Series: **Animal Planet**